KRASNOYARSK

LAKE
BAIKAL

KHABAROVSK

IRKUTSK

NAKHODKA

ANGARA RIVER

SEA OF

JAPAN

ANOTHER SIDE TO RUSSIA

ANOTHER SIDE TO RUSSIA

JUNE KELLY

Published by David Bateman

To my husband Bob who only lost me once

ACKNOWLEDGEMENTS

The 'INTOURIST' Russian travel organisation who always did their best

492-87

© June Kelly 1985
First published by David Bateman Ltd
Buderim, Queensland 4556, Australia

National Library of Australia
Cataloguing-in-Publication data

  Kelly, June
    Another Side to Russia

    ISBN 0 908610 51 3

    1. Kelly, June. 2. Drawing, Australian.
    3. Soviet Union in art. 4. Painting,
    Australian. 5. Flowers in art. I. Title.

0S
741.994

Printed in Hong Kong

CONTENTS

Introduction

When Bob, my husband, and I decided to visit Russia I never expected it would be the subject of my third book. To me, Russia had always conjured up visions of Cathedrals with onion-shaped domes, parades in Red Square and barren plains that turn into snow-scapes in the winter.

So it was with a less than open mind that we arrived on the Russian ferry *M.V. Baikal* at the eastern port of Nakhoda to start the Trans-Siberian railway part of our trip. We were only able to glimpse briefly the picturesque and busy harbour before being confined to our cabins where we were told to remain until the ferry berthed. This experience, and the slow Customs clearance, was our first taste of Russian officialdom. However, I must say the Intourist Organisation, which is the only tourist organisation foreigners can use, was remarkably efficient and functioned smoothly — sometimes too smoothly, as often we would have welcomed some spare time!

The first leg of our long train journey was to be to Khabarovsk and it was on this stretch that I startled the two young carriage attendants, and worried our guide Tanya, by taking out my sketch book and starting to draw an old station building. The reason for such concern, I suppose, was our proximity to the Chinese border and military

6

installations. Tanya, our official guide who accompanied us throughout the trip, always seemed to be watching what I was drawing but, eventually, I think she realised I didn't pose a security risk!

As the journey progressed, I began to realise there was another side to Russia; the landscape was green and soft, there were forests of silver birch and, to my absolute delight, wild flowers in profusion. There were occasions when I had the opportunity to pick flowers and place them in a plastic bag. I would soak them in water in the hotel bathroom, and, later paint them at my leisure aboard the train.

It was this side of Russia with its flowers, old churches and rural population that inspired me to put my sketches and impressions into a book. I have sketched the journey and, for those who would like to pinpoint the places we visited, I have drawn a route map for the endpapers. At the end of it all, I had enough notes and sketches to fill five books. So, if there are readers who have been to Russia and feel I have omitted somewhere of importance, please forgive me.

I would love to return to Russia — but without a guide — and spend more time exploring some of the interesting towns and cities off the beaten tourist track.

I hope my drawings and paintings show that there is Another Side to Russia.

Our first stop was the city of Khabarovsk on the banks of the Amur River and a familiarisation tour of the city was the first item on the day's itinerary. Andrei was our guide for the day; an enthusiastic student rapt in the achievements of Communism and the city's monuments. I only had time to sketch three of them as we sped past many lovely old buildings.

Monument to the Civil War Heroes

Monument to the Second World War Heroes

Monument to
Yerofei Khabarov

Later, we were allowed to stroll around the city and this formal fountain caught my eye. Russian boys, it seems, also have time to play with water. The bedding dahlias were in spring flower in the city squares. I think they had been raised in a greenhouse as they were placed in the beds in pots.

The train passed by many small communes. But, on this occasion, it stopped behind these little houses. Out came my sketch book. All were built from logs with slabs of wood for roofs and, like all the communes we saw, each had a small vegetable plot with potatoes and climbing beans.

Then a delay for two hours so I joined others who had left the train to pick flowers; the carriage attendants anxiously watched the engine ahead, as part of their job was to make sure no-one got left behind. Toadflax grew everywhere alongside the tracks.

Forests of silver birch and swathes of rose bay willow herb stretched for many miles. Sometimes, although there were no visible signs of habitation, small potato patches could be seen in what seemed to be the middle of nowhere.

Museum of
Local Law
Small windows Irkutsh
enhanced the red brick
walls.

Lilac trees in
flower and
quaint cottages with
picket fences
Lake Baikal

Blue shutters

I couldn't help but admire
this decoratively carved
window frame.

At Irkutsk, early in the morning, we were whisked by coach from the train to the Intourist Hotel. After a shower, there was still time to explore before breakfast. My memories are of tree-shaded streets which formed a green framework for the buildings and this lovely old gateway. Opposite are sketches of some fascinating windows in the city.

We were taken to Lake Baikal by bus and could see the blue water long before we got there. It's the deepest lake in the world, over 1400 feet above sea level, and fed by more than 300 tributary rivers tumbling from the mountainsides which stretch around the lake as far as the eye can see.

Before the railway was built through the southern mountains, a British built combined ferry boat and ice breaker carried the trains across. During the Russo/Japanese war this caused a bottleneck as only three trains could be ferried daily each way. In winter, rails were laid on the ice and wagons were hauled across by horses.

Masses of wild flowers covered the ground. I've painted just a few of them, geraniums, dianthus, clovers, buttercups, and the guide told us there were hundreds of species around the lake not found anywhere else in the world.

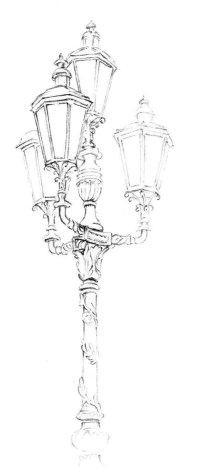

I was captivated by the many different lamp standards throughout Russia — this one was more ornate than most. I suppose they were used in the rest of the world until technology replaced them with neon lights. Not all the lighting in Russia was as lovely as this. I suspect these are still being used for purely functional economic reasons rather than for their beauty. This low-growing variety of campanula looked so dainty amongst the taller grasses.

Campanula
poscharshyana

The unusual colour of this timber restaurant on the shore of Lake Baikal made it an interesting subject. I put my head round the door and it seemed full of Russian fishermen. Unfortunately, it was not on the Intourist list of eating places for I think I would have enjoyed a meal there. People everywhere appeared to accept our presence, but with no obvious signs of pleasure — a sort of distant politeness.

I found this typical timber building in the old part of the city of Irkutsk. These fascinating houses with their intricately carved features appeared to be falling into disrepair. I gathered the impression that anything old was being rejected and replaced with concrete apartment blocks devoid of national character. But I don't think this only happens in Russia.

The flower is wild chicory.

Everywhere, I was
enthralled by the beautifully
designed domes and towers
on churches and buildings.
This sweet william seemed
to complement the sketches.

23

24

This was the view from our ninth floor corner suite of the hotel in Irkutsk. I just had to paint the warm, mellow old building in the morning light. The nasturtiums and lobelia were growing in pots on nearby balconies. The feeling was almost Mediterranean.

Eastern border station

1959

Wild strawberry

Intourists on the train had access to the dining car but Russian travellers carried their own food and must have appreciated these station stalls. I must mention the sheer efficiency of the Trans-Siberian railway. It seemed to us that trains were slotted about 8 minutes apart, 24 hours a day, in each direction, carrying people, cars, troops, timber, gasoline and general freight.

Station vendors with bucket of berries.

Old an

No overnight stops between Irkutsk and Moscow meant four days on the train with just short breaks of about 20 minutes at the major stations. But long enough for a quick sketch. I've re-drawn a number of these stations with some of the flowers growing alongside the tracks.

Siberian station, timber construction.

Perm.

Yaroslavski Terminal Moscow

Old engine with three carriages at ... Whistled & chuffed off

We crossed the Urals which seemed more like rolling hills than mountains, and glimpsed the obelisk marking the border between Europe and Asia. Next came the steppes which were, perhaps, the 'longest' part of this marvellous trip. Vast open lands with just a small commune every now and then.

Black currants

Then the scenery changed
to forests and this was
reflected by the number
of log trains travelling
east.

At each station there
were stalls with fresh
vegetables and fruit.
Sometimes peasant
women stood with buckets
containing paper screws
of berries and,
occasionally, flowers such
as gladioli.

Siberian ox-eye daisies and an unusual groundcover grew under shrubby trees near the duck pond, but I've not been able find the name of the other pretty plant. The wooden building was just one of several at the Museum of Wooden Structures in Suzdal. Some have been moved there and others created in the old style. Bluebells and wood hyacinths were everywhere. Despite delays for track maintenance and repair, our train arrived in Moscow only seven minutes late.

But before we had a chance to look around, we were rushed by motorcoach 160 miles to Suzdal and Vladimir. Halfway, we stopped for lunch at this Intourist Restaurant. Although quite new, it was built in the old style using large, heavy timbers and logs.

Wood Hyacinths

Wood was used in early architecture in many countries. In Russia it developed into a remarkable artform. For instance, this 17th century church was constructed without a single nail.

Much of the early work was done with axes and the decorative details were finished with saws, drills and chisels. Even peasant homes reflected the skill of the woodcutter's art. Sadly, in the 19th century the fashion was to cover the log buildings with board facings like those on the two old windmills.

This is the Golden Gate in Vladimir. In 1157, Andrei Bogolyubski was Grand Prince of Vladimir, Suzdal and Rostov, but he abandoned Suzdal and made Vladimir the capital of Russia. He encircled the town with a wooden wall and constructed this Golden Gate in the western side facing Moscow which was then a small village. The rounded bastions were added much later but the tiny chapel perched above is part of the original gate.

A tree-shaded lane led to this 12th century Cathedral of the Assumption. I drew it framed by a sprig of red berries from a rowan tree.

35

Suzdal, on the Kamenkia River, boasts five monasteries and fifty churches. The Russians often built a large church for summer and a smaller, heated one for winter. In the foreground of this picture is the winter church with the summer one behind.

Whilst in Suzdal, I also painted the church on the title page of this book. Like so many, it was locked. The octagonal belfry caught my eye — how I would have loved to go inside.

This house stood out from those around it, neatly painted in dark red and white. I tried to find out who lived in it — but, no luck — and no explanation as to why this one was so well kept. All the houses, no matter how small, had huge piles of wood in readiness for the winter. Wild daisies and other flowers seemed to flourish everywhere beside the pathways. No mown lawns here.

Borders of petunias led to the
Cathedral of the Nativity inside the
Suzdal kremlin. Kremlin was a word I
got used to in Russia — it actually
means fort or fortress.

That night, 18 hours and 320 miles
later, we returned to Moscow, worn
out.

Next morning we set off for Red Square. At one end stands
St Basil's Cathedral, now a museum, built by Ivan the
Terrible between 1554 and 1560. It commemorates the
annexation by Russia of Kazan and Astrakan. It was intended
to be the most beautiful cathedral in Russia; as I first saw it,
over the bright red tulips, I am sure it is.

The Spassky Tower, part of the Kremlin, was built 70 years earlier by Italian craftsmen. It's from here, on the hour every hour, that high-stepping ceremonial guards take their places at the entrance to Lenin's Mausoleum.

The first Kremlin was a wooden fort completed in 1156. Its oak log walls were replaced in 1367 by white stones. In the late 15th century, when the Russians freed themselves from the Tartars, Ivan the Third emerged as the first Czar and it was then that the red brick walls and towers replaced the white stones. The Kremlin has changed very little since those days.

Here I show some of the domes and spires of various shapes and colours which surmount the complex of chapels.

The Czar camellia grows well throughout Russia as it does in the rest of the world. It's a great favourite with camellia growers.

St Basil's is also known as the
Pokrovsky Cathedral. It was called St
Basil's after Basil, the Russian holy
fool who was 'idiotic for Christ's
sake' and who was buried in the
church's vaults. It was designed by
two Russian architects, Postnik and
Barma and not, as popular legend has
it by an Italian who was blinded so he
could never create anything like it, or
its equal, ever again.

The 'Tsar Kolokol' (King of Bells) is the largest known bell in the world. It weighs 193 tons, is 19 feet high and has never been rung! In 1737, fire destroyed its supports and it fell, an 11 ton piece breaking off from its side.

Not far away, the Tsar's cannon, like the huge bell, is an accolade to the foundry skills of that time. Cast in 1586, the barrel is over 17 feet and has a calibre of 3 feet. The cast iron cannon balls are purely decorative for it has never been fired.

Czar Cannon 1586

Tourists enter the Kremlin through the Borovitsky Gate where keen-eyed guards make sure that only cameras are brought in. Cannas were growing not far away. In Russian, the word 'red' also means 'beautiful' and I certainly saw more red flowers than any other colour.

Nine golden domes decorate the Cathedral of the Annunciation, completed in 1489 on the site of an old church first built in 1397. An Aladdin-like building, delicate and graceful — but we were not given time to go inside.

Moscow's Bolshoi Theatre, built in neo-classical style, has replaced the original building which was destroyed by fire. It is the home of the Bolshoi Ballet. Bolshoi means 'big ballet' in Russian. It is the leading company in the Soviet Union, renowned for its elaborately staged classic and children's ballets. The Ballet was established in 1825 when the Bolshoi Theatre took over the Petrovsky Theatre. Because of heavy bookings, sadly, Bob and I were unable to see the world famous ballet, but we were content to go to one of the lesser ballets which we thoroughly enjoyed.

Rhododendrons grow wild here but I saw these cultivated in a park. They seemed to complement the beauty of the architecture.

We left Moscow late one evening for our overnight trip to Leningrad.

Leningrad was the last
place we visited. Full of
wonderful buildings, it
possesses so much beauty.
There are many fountains
in the parks around Peter
the Great's Summer
Palace, the roof of which I
have sketched in the
background.

Some impressions around Leningrad
from an intourist coach

Monolith in Palace Square.
Commemorates victory over
Napoleon in 1812.
Survived the siege in
Second World War.

Leningrad was the capital of the
Russian Empire from 1712 to 1918.
So much to see, and so little time.

*Lamp posts of
many designs.*

Lilac

*Bridges over canals
with decorative iron railings*

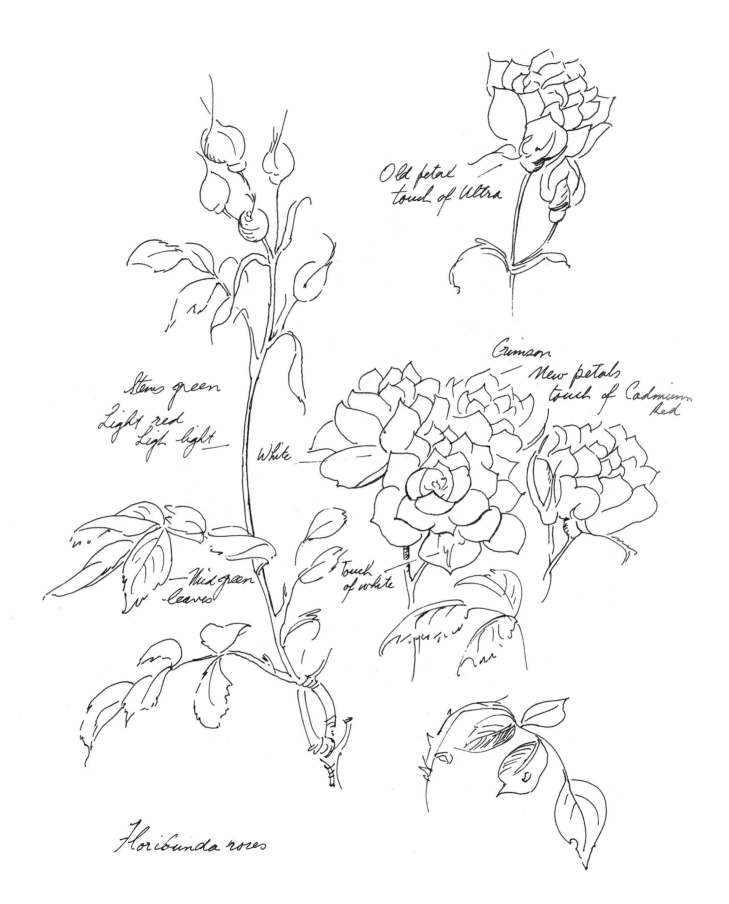

Old petal
touch of Ultra

Crimson
New petals
touch of Cadmium
Red

Stems green
Light red
Light light

White

Mid green
leaves

Touch
of white

Floribunda roses

54

One of the gateways to the Summer Gardens which were ablaze with floribunda roses. The Summer Palace is 18 miles from Leningrad. It was destroyed during World War II but was one of the first buildings to be re-constructed in its original form. It's a pleasant place to stroll and my painting is done from these working sketches.

St Isaac's Cathedral is the largest church in
Leningrad, an imposing sight with its tall gilt dome.
Now a museum, its interior is opulent with white
marble and gilded mosaic icons.